He Talks in Tongues

Tracilyn George

©2018 Tracilyn George

Contents

AFTERMATH 6

CONDEMNATION..7

HURRICANE 8

STORM..9

FROM HERE TO THERE 11

MIDNIGHT MUSK 12

GHOST TOWN 13

LE CAFÉ DE LES BLUES....................................14

WHAT HAPPENS TO US?....................................15

HEARTACHE 17

WONDERING...19

FINE WITH ME 21

STREETS OF TIME 23

DECISIONS 25

THE BAR 27

CRIMINAL..29

HEARTLESS 30

BATTLEFIELD...32

WAR..33

HEAT OF PASSION...34

HE LOOKS AT ME	36
ABDUCTION	38
JEOPARDY	39
STALKER	40
THE RAPE	41
MANIPULATORS	42
UNHOLY VAGABOND	43
MASSACRE	44
HE TALKS IN TONGUES	45
THE CAVERN	46
IN SHAMBLES	47
MASQUERADE	48
BURGLAR	49
APPARITION	50
MOB KILLING	51
DEATH	52
CHILD	53
LOVE STRUCK	54
MY HEART BLEEDS	56
SOLICITOR	57
THE EXECUTION OF TED	58

AFTERMATH

Darkness comes
No will to live
Unending depression
No crying
No laughing
Nothing
Emotionless
Staring into space
Silent pleas for help
No one hears
For no one cares
Deeper and deeper
I fall into myself
I reach out
But no one's around
Death makes sense
No fear
No pain
Farewell
Forever

CONDEMNATION

Grey skies loom
Heavily overhead
Ominously whispering
Their words of condemnation.
Wild winds whistle
Through threadbare trees
Screaming sinister threats
And uttering their condemnation.
Dogs, once dormant
Wail forlornly
In the distance
Howling menacingly
Their views and condemnation.
Feral cats hiss
Screeching hatefully
In run-down alleys
Squealing hideously
Their sneers and condemnation.
Birds of prey
Soar as the unsavory vultures they are
Squawking loudly
Lying in wait
To spew their condemnation.

HURRICANE

Cold freezing rain
Splashes against the window.
Harsh winds crash the defenseless glass.
Friendless black clouds
Take control of the dark sky.
Stripped trees swing
Their naked branches furiously.
Leaves, brown and withered,
Swirl evilly on the ground.
Birds huddle together, frightened and cold.
Squirrels scurry to find shelter
Against the storm.
Almost instantly, it intensifies,
Throwing branches at everything.
Angry and fierce,
Its wrath upon all
For no reason apparent.
Its purpose unknown,
Destruction its only defense,
Leaving many dead
Injured
And stranded,
With nowhere to go
And nowhere to turn.

STORM

Fog weaves and
Winds around
Darkened trees while
Bushes sway slightly
In the cool
Autumn air.
Gulls of the sea
Flock along
The rancid beaches
In search of nourishment.
Grey storm clouds
Stalk a beautiful girl.
Her once ivory
Flawless skin
Reflected a harsh
Unrewarding life.
An emptiness
A void of love
And of attention.
Her pale blue eyes
Mirrors a nothingness
That was so prominent
In her short life.
A father who left
When she was but a
Tender age of three.
A mother who passed on
A few short months later.
Foster home
To foster home,

The young girl was tossed;
Battered and bruised
Stumbling through a
War-torn
Ongoing struggle
For a bluer sky.
The bleakest of nights
Dominate her life now
As she pushes her way
Through the storm
To a point
Where life seems
A mere existence.

FROM HERE TO THERE

From here,
There seems so far away
So confused
So lost.
From here,
There seems a bitter place,
Being torn away
At the seams.
Here trying its best
To get there
All sewn up.
But here
To there
Seems just as lost
Confused
And bitter
From there.
Here is being torn
From the inside out.
Here and there
Cannot help
What is going on.
There and here
Until they cure
What is going on
Inside the hearts
Of everyone
Everywhere.

MIDNIGHT MUSK

Shadowy figures flee.
Moonlight illuminates.
Dark alleys cover.
Trash cans crash.
Strays wail.
Tires screech.
Policeman's whistle.
Conmen hustle.
Victims moan.
Streetlamps flutter
Televisions buzz.
Windows alight.
Fathers grumble.
Mothers scream.
Children whine.
Taxis fly.
Bums roam.
Garbage idle.
Glass breaks.
Alarms ring.
Sirens sound.
Robbers run.
People hide.
Ambulances rush.
Relatives gush
With the pungent odor
Of the
Midnight musk.

GHOST TOWN

Brown barren land
Covered with grass
Withered and dead.
The sun was gray
As ere the darkened clouds around it.
Grey colorless waves
Fell coldly upon the beach,
Void of people and livestock
Deserted and empty.
Pieces of wood
From a wrecked abandoned vessel
Floated upon the shore.
A chill wind whistled
Through the empty trees
Undying
Increasing as it passes.
Sand flew overhead
Mixed with frigid rain.
Houses worn and ragged
Deserted and quiet
Boarded up
As their owners
Restless
Leave for the city.

LE CAFÉ DE LES BLUES

In a dark
Dingy quarter of Paris
Stands a rundown
And dirty café
Where the loneliest
Most depress souls
Meet for near-cold coffee
And month-old croissants.
At Le Café de les Blues,
There is an air
Of gloominess,
So permanent
In time
It stands,
A lonely
Dismal place to stay.
For the restless,
The unattached
And the unwanted.
All are welcome
To share in their misery,
To wallow in their pain.
Le Café stands unstable;
Its only source
Of stability
Are the comings
Of the loneliest
Most depressed souls.

WHAT HAPPENS TO US?

What happens to us
When our love
Fades away?
Do we become two?
Just me?
Just you?
Or do we become
You and I
Together
As friends
But apart
As lovers?
What happens to us
When our hearts
Just aren't in it?
Do we just split apart?
Like the heartless amoeba?
Set off driftless
In no particular direction?
What happens to us
When we just can't
Seem to get along?
Do we part
As enemies?
Warriors trying to prove
They are the superior?
What happens to us
When our love
Becomes too strong?
Do we sizzle

With each other
Until our fire's
Near burnt out?
What happens to us
If we just
Seem to click?
Do we try it?
Do we even dare
To take the chance?
What happens to us
If we can't get up?
Do we hustle?
Do we bustle?
Just to quench
Our needs?

HEARTACHE

The moment that
Discovered your love
Was not for me;
My heart
It sank
To the bottom
Of the sea.
The pain
I felt
That dreary day
Is a pin
I know
Will never go away.
On my sleeve
It seems to stay
To be hurt again
Some other way.
Heartache will be
My way of life.
Always there
Like piercing knives.
It is my will
That keeps me strong.
It's the only thing
That keeps me going.
My heart aches
Because of you
Of you alone.
To you
I send my broken heart

That away you've thrown.
So mighty
You act
When you are with her
But I know
Deep down
That it's she you fear.
Now I leave you
With your broad
And I shall live
Above you, love.

WONDERING

I walk
Through the rain
A warm soothing
Yet unresting rain.
As I walk
Through this rain
I wonder
About the doings
Of our troubled world.
Throughout the centuries
There has rarely
Been peace.
Once things start
To look up
For us,
A country
Would attack
To stir up
The world.
From the ancient Greeks
And Egyptians
To modern day life.
Every country
Has been in war.
Within itself
Or against others.
In the past century alone,
We've had
The Boer War
The War to end all wars;

The Second World War
Korea
Vietnam,
The Attack on Pearl Harbor
Iraq versus Iran
Czechoslovakia
Romania
Plus, countless others.
Now the Persian Gulf Crisis
With Iraq
Invading Kuwait
And I wander
Wondering why
Everyone wants
To control
Everyone and everything else.
And I wonder why
People cannot
Settle things peacefully.
But it seems
Like the whole world
Is so gung-ho
About guns and ammunition
And nuclear weapons.
Then I wonder
If they weren't
How boring
Peace on earth
Would be.

FINE WITH ME

Tell me that
You love me
Or tell me
That you don't.
Either way
Is fine with me
My son.
Tell me that
You'll stay
Or tell me
That you'll go
'Cause baby
Either way
Is fine,
You know.
Tell me if
You want me
Or tell me
If you don't.
Again, you know
Is fine by me
And tell me if
You need me
Or tell me if
You don't.
That's quite alright
With me.
Do you lust me
Or do you not?
Baby,

All I'm saying
Is to tell me
Either way.

STREETS OF TIME

Through the heartless
Streets of time,
I walk alone
In search of
Everlasting tranquility.
And as I walk
These streets of time,
I think of all
That has happened
In my short
Unhappy lifetime.
My parents' deaths,
my brother's murder,
My uncle raping me.
I also remember
The cruelty of the village children
Intentional
And unintentional,
Their harsh words
Stinging more so
Than their beatings.
Their parents seem
Almost as cruel
By ignoring their children's actions.
These streets of time
Get so cold at times.
Sometimes the day
Is more frigid
Than the night
For at night,

The crickets sing to me
To an almost peaceful slumber.
It is almost warming
Comforting
To hear them chirp.
They have taken
The place
Of my mother's voice;
Of her warm arms
Holding me closely
After an intense nightmare.
They are my family now
These crickets
And the streets.
The cold empty streets of time
Seem to stretch on
Forever
Into a distant horizon
Which never seems
To have an end.
Yet I always seem
To strive for
And never reach
This paradise.

DECISIONS

Here
I sit
Alone
In my thoughts,
Wondering
Wandering
Through memories
When times
Were simple,
Uncomplicated
When the biggest decision
To be made
Was who would be it
In a game of tag.
But now
Life altering choices
Play their hand.
To stay
In a place
Where I will
Never be happy
Or leave,
Taking a chance
That I may
Find pace
Contentment
Or at least
A glimmer
Of hope.
Here

I sit
Watching
The sun fade
To a distant memory.
The decision
Dawns on me
To take myself
To a better place
So at least
I would have
The chance
To make
More decisions.

THE BAR

The bright, pink sunset
Transforms into a dark, blackish night.
No moon nor stars
Not even a twinkle
From the dim, dreary streetlamps.
A solitary girl
Walks quietly along the pavement.
She passes a loud, well-lit pub
Music blaring and drunken men
Brawling and searing
Yelling vulgarities at the poor barmaids.
Carefully,
Daintily,
With a slight curiosity
The girl takes a step inside.
The sudden brightness
Almost blinding her
Temporarily making her vulnerable
Rude whistles filter through the air
Reaching her tender ears and reddening her cheeks.
Her slender waist making her supple breasts look larger.
Her pale ivory complexion with fain freckles
Framed lightly by titan locks
Confusion and amazement
In her violet eyes
As the drunkards pinch her
And make crude passes at her.
Frustrated tears fill her eyes

She tries to push her way out.
Her clothes and body becoming ripped
And disheveled in the process.
Her breath becomes heavy
As she runs aimlessly through the streets
Until she reaches the security
Of her porch
Lit only by a single lamp.

CRIMINAL

He slips into the darkness
Followed only by his own black shadow;
Accompanied by his guilty conscious
And a cool hundred million in cash.
He tiptoes around the underbrush
So not to arouse the unsuspecting wilderness.
He runs swiftly through the trees
With nowhere to turn
With no courage to go back.
He hop-scotches across the uplifted roots
Jumping over small boulders
Heading aimlessly to anywhere the path leads him,
Eager to discover a cavern to camouflage his body.
He continues to flee through the blackness,
The fear of being caught filtering through his skin
As he heads for the end of the trees
Towards the light of the distant city
But as he steps into the emptiness
He is surrounded by policemen and agents
Unwilling to give up their claim.

HEARTLESS

You are
So heartless.
You waltz
Into my life,
Rip out my heart
Then walk off
With no guilt
Whatsoever.
You leave me
With nothing
But an emptiness
That you only can fill.
I am not ashamed
To admit that
I need you
So desperately.
I feel worthless
Without you here.
I am so empty
Without you
In my arms
Dancing the night away.
Yet you are
So heartless
You want to please
Only yourself.
You do not are
Who you hurt
In the process.
I know

For I am guilty
Of the same.
My darling
Can you possibly
Understand what
I am saying?
Or what
You are doing?
I doubt it
For if you did
You would stay
With me
Forever.

BATTLEFIELD

Chimes ring ceremoniously through
The crisp autumn air as
Troops of soldiers are paraded
Through the littered streets
As masses of hero worshipers
Line the rubbish-filled alleys
To catch a glimpse of the men
Who battled and served overseas
In order to protect their country's honor
And allow them to keep their freedom.
As the forces march past the slums
Of the lower class and mentally disabled
Dark and monstrous clouds overtake
The cold November day,
Ominously threatening a frigid downpour
And as the rain teems upon
The black and grimy streets,
It is the group of servicemen who run
And seek for cover
For what they hear is not thunder
But the roar of shells.

WAR

Cold, lonely darkness falls
Like rain upon the empty earth.
Children roam the street
Begging for food
Begging for shelter
And begging for love.
Empty liquor bottles clutter the house
As wives with blackened eyes scream
And fight against their drunken husbands.
I sit and watch the rain for hours,
Thinking of nothing but the hardships
And I wonder what this world is coming to.
Why we thrive on such violence.
It excites us
Makes our hearts pound
Our blood boil.
It's as if we can't survive without it
And many die because of it.
Our rulers just pass it off
Saying that death is
Just a natural part of living.
It isn't fair
But we don't do anything about it
As darkness falls upon an empty world
And the earth is enveloped in silence.

HEAT OF PASSION

In her steely eyes
Flash a heated anger
As she walks
Undaunted
Unafraid towards her victim
Unknowing of
Her fury;
Unaware of
How truly
How deep
Her rage runs
Within her.
Her wrath comes.
From so much torture
So much pain
Over weeks of
Assumed passion.
Subtle mind games
He played with her,
Toying
With her heart
With her emotions
Making public
Yet indistinct put-downs
Around her,
Causing the maiden
To feel inferior
Unwanted
Unworthy.
She is so

Crazed with anger
That she
Is willing
To put her life
On the line
To put
An end
To his.

HE LOOKS AT ME

He looks at me
With lust
In his eyes.
His intentions
Far from honorable.
His heart
Far from pure.
He looks at me
With lusts.
His hands
Wanting more.
He looks at me
With lust
In his eyes.
His groin
On fire.
His stomach
Churning.
He looks at me
With lust
In his eyes.
His hands
Wanting more.
His body
Aching.
He looks at me
With lust
In his eyes.
His intentions
Far from honorable.

His heart
Far from pure.

ABDUCTION

Through the harsh African foliage,
A mischievous male treks the unwalked paths,
Searching for his beloved childhood sweetheart,
Abducted by her venomous stepfather.
He pushes through the thick jungle,
Fury and passion urging him on,
Guiding him to the depths of Africa
Where his beautiful darling lady
Was held by ropes and chains
And brutally beaten by her father.
In a blind rage,
The man
Strong and godlike,
Rips through the fragile hut,
Sending it into countless shreds
And with an angry, silent blow
Knocks the father into hell.

JEOPARDY

The darkened sky loomed
Over a turbulent sea.
A young man's reddened face
Was pale despite the fact.
He followed his angered captain's orders,
Staying fast at his post.
The vicious waves were beating
Fiercely against the ship
As the mighty sailors
Were weakened by the illness.
Some so craze with fever
Had dared to overboard jump.
The best of the best
Of these men
Were no match
Against the elements.
The gods were testing them
Or so it seemed
As many good men
Went down with their ship.

STALKER

Darkness filters through
The partially exposed window.
The dim moon is covered
By a black misty blanket.
A dark-hooded shadow
Creeps ominously through the alleys.
A disgusted scowl escapes his lips
As a stray cat darts in front of him.
He growls
Stroking his beloved blade.
His presence is almost overbearing
Sending a chill through everyone present.
His eyes were of blue ice
Freezing one's soul
Electrifying
Almost paralyzing
They dart nervously
Evilly
Stalking his prey
Wit the perfection
Of a cheetah.
With impeccable ease
And a flick of the wrist
He slashes her throat.
He leaves her
Bleeding profusely
As he goes
To stalk
Another victim.

THE RAPE

Clouds float slowly
Over an orange moon
As chill winds
Whistle through naked trees.
A dark shadow
Creeps up behind.
A shrill scream
Hands pulling roughly
Tugging
Ripping
Tearing at clothing
Pushing himself on her.
Dark corners hide
The evil close by,
Haunting spells surround
Eerie spirits command
As battered figures
Come out for revenge.

MANIPULATORS

A dire haze rises from
The cold murky heath
As a ghostly silhouette trudges
Noiselessly through the moor.
His superficial body drifts
Restlessly upon the misty earth.
His gray empty eyes reveal
A piercing fiendlike past
When his now silver colored hair
Was a dark auburn hue.
An icy shadow dominates
The black noiseless scene.
Evil winds whistle frigidly
Through frozen ebony frames
Of dark deserted and dingy dumps
Once occupied by wealthy
Powerful men of authority
Manipulating and plundering
And ravishing to achieve.
Privileges and stature undeserving
Of the sub rose attributes,
Thrashing their wives
Seducing their whores
Bringing commoners to their knees
Robbing them of everything they own
And stripping them of their values.

UNHOLY VAGABOND

As winds whirl around
Swirling around dust
A raven-haired girl floats
Over the cobblestone streets.
Her deep lapis eyes reflect
A cold hard nothingness,
An emptiness brought on
By an endless poverty
And a long forever abuse
From her father and her brothers.
She walks timidly through
The small English village
Her long, ebony tresses flowing
In the cool autumn breeze
As she wanders aimlessly
Forever upon the ancient boulevards
With her face ashen and blotched
Beaten by her family
Rejected by the public.
She roams eternally
In search of
Everlasting tranquility.

MASSACRE

Icy breezes caress
And cradle
Barren bushes
As crumpled leaves
Dance playfully
Among the ivy.
Tiny squirrels
Chatter noisily
In the birches.
Rocks crunch
Under children's feet
As they crack
Small twigs
While playing tag.
A loud shot
Fills the air
Sharp
Crisp
Accurate
Then
Innocent infants
Are laid to rest.

HE TALKS IN TONGUES

He talks in tongues, like the gurus
Of ancient times and modern cults
And all the blackness of the night
Comes seeping through his eyes;
Thus, leaving the world
Mysteriously under his spell.
One more follower, one believer less
As they follow customs of the past.
Children of this new-found god
Sacrifice their hard-earned lives;
But, once they realize that he's fake
By then, it's just far too late.
Unlike his heroes from before,
The guru now is after more
Than your favors and your faith;
A man like him wants your pay.
So, take care, all my comrades
Guys like that are all bad.

THE CAVERN

A blackened haze surrounds
The dark mountain
As a crow swoops evilly
Around its icy base.
A small boy is trapped
Within a snow-filled cavern,
His leg broken and bloody.
His weepy cries echo out
To no avail.
He pulls himself to a rock
Collapsing weakly upon
Its smooth slimy surface,
His wound becoming worse
Turning a sickly blue.
His face transforms
To a white disfigurement of pain.
His breathing becomes short and breathless.
Vomiting continuously upon the earth,
He groans
Weakening.
The illness and infection
Taking its toll upon the boy.
He falls
Gasping for air.
His eyes become glazed
Then empty
As life slips
Out of his frail body.

IN SHAMBLES

Quiet
She lies
Upon her bed
Staring
At the ceiling.
Her heart
In shambles
Beyond repair.
The man
She adores
Went off to war
Leaving her
Alone
And five months
With child.
Quiet
She lies
Upon her bed
Staring
At the ceiling.
The child
Near due
Makes its presence known.
She moans
In minor discomfort.
Her heart
In shambles
Knowing the baby
Will never truly know
Its father.

MASQUERADE

Through the heavy fog
Walks a pale silhouette.
Her face
White as an Easter lily
Is empty
Disguising
Her inner torment
Her anger
Her pain.
The memories
Of the abuse
And her father
So large
So heavy
Upon her
And then the stranger
So hard
So rough
Towards her.
Consequently
She lives
Her life
Behind the mask.

BURGLAR

Screams fill the electric air
As thunder crashes
And lightning flashes.
Ominous shadows creep
And crawl around the darkness.
Torrents of water beat against
Threadbare habitations.
Grimy tramps beg
And sleep among the trash.
A black silhouette
Moves along the shadows
Undaunted by the sirens
As he creeps through
The crowded dirt-filled alleys.
He crashes a window
Of a nearby store,
Setting off its silent alarm.
His hands bloodied
Dripping onto his clothes
As the police handcuff
And drag him away.

APPARITION

Murky fog hovers eerily
Over a sleepless tomb
As an unresting apparition
Floats across the empty grave
Endlessly searching for peace
Restlessly roaming the frigid earth
Untiring of its long, unending mission
Of forever and tranquil slumber.
Throughout eternal time
It travels
Passing through periods
Walking through territories.
Its ageless being flies
Adrift upon the moors.
It sees its family living
And growing prosperously
Content
Knowing that they are well
Vanishes into non-existence.

MOB KILLING

Blood painted the streets.
Black clouds covered the sky,
Looming angrily over the city.
Policemen attacked the scene
As bums pass by
Unaffected by the sight.
The victim
Major mob leader in the area
Drug dealer and pimp
A real ladies' man, one said.
Killed by a ruthless, vengeful opponent,
A loan shark, probably
Another pimp or drug boss
Jealous of his success.
The cops mused long and hard
Over the multiple possibilities
But in the end
Left it closed
As an unsolvable case.

DEATH

Lightning flashes through the air.
All of nature does despair.
As thunder crashes upon the earth
Even the insects search for shelter.
The rain pours throughout the world
Drenching and quenching the thirsty foliage.
Shadows rule the darkened land
As a quiet figure strides along
Seemingly unaware of his predicament.
Blood gushes from his face
And from his hands.
His clothes soaked and grimy
Ripped and worn from time.
He is black, almost indistinguishable.
His face so dirty and unfamiliar
Yet his presence is usual.
Death is prominent.
He waits patiently for his number
As the blackened clouds surround
The overbearing and angry moon.
But as he rises above the earth
The storms become a forgotten nightmare.

CHILD

Images
Of a forgotten love
Flow through her heart
Through her soul.
She shakes it off
To think of him
Her new joy
Her baby boy
Given to her
By a street-wise gangster
Who held her at gunpoint.
She smiles
As her child gurgles
And laughs
In the next room.
She kneels to play
And pray for her baby
As her long-lost love
Strolls evilly towards him.

LOVE STRUCK

A blackened highway
Stretches into empty nothingness.
A lone figure travels
Its long, charcoal asphalt
Roaming forever
Throughout unending eternity
Furiously searching for
His long, forsaken lover.
So insanely infatuated with her
So long forlorn for her
He walks eternally upon the highway
In hopes of one day finding her
Waiting for him with open arms
To greet him tenderly.
Under starry skies and a yellow moon
His stride quickens
In anticipation
And the excitement
Of his dream.
His blue eyes brighten;
Eyes that were once
Dead and empty
And a body which
Once was old and disintegrating
Now is young and vibrant
Full of life and
Void of hopelessness and age.
As he travels the
Long, black highway,
He is unseen

By an oncoming vehicle
Traveling swiftly
And uncaring
Towards him.

MY HEART BLEEDS

Because of you
My heart bleeds.
It longs to have
You by my side.
It bleeds because
You just
Up and left
Without a reason;
Without a word
Breaking it
Into many pieces.
So fragmented
It will never be
Whole again.
Because of you
My heart
Will never love
Again.

SOLICITOR

As the world slips into
An intense and frozen blackness,
The dark abandoned streets
Are occupied by an unsociable
And unsightly masculine figure
Wandering aimlessly among
The wailing strays and sleeping tramps
In quest of lodgings and
A tender passionate maiden
Wanting a companion
To share a life together.
As he travels alone
Endlessly
Tirelessly
Through time
Seemingly never to find a lover,
He falls into the hands
Of an unsympathetic officer
Who in turn
Arrests and imprisons him
For procuring and soliciting.

THE EXECUTION OF TED

Darkness falls heavily upon the empty streets
Half-past midnight and no one in sight.
A lone figure strolls along the black pavement
His face emotionless under the pale moon
Even his pale brown eyes are empty.
The long, sinewy fingers of his blood-stained hands
Reach unknowingly into the blackness.
His victims lie stripped and bloody
Dying or dead in darkness and out of view.
The houses surrounding him stand quiet
Large and ominous as he passes slowly.
His head and mind are in a daze,
An uncontrollable evil frenzy.
Two a.m. and he's sitting alone on a bunk
In a cell with several guards on the outside.
He still holds the unemotional look.
His eyes are silent, blankly staring
Into the empty moonlight streaming in.
The mothers of victims sleep uneasily,
Hatred and anger showing in their bloodshot eyes.
Six-thirty, the man is preparing for the end.
His face is clean, his eyes full of nothingness.
He paces the floor with unusual ease.
He is peculiarly calm and strangely unnerved.
At seven, he is pushed through concrete corridors
To a dark, silent room with only a single chair
Wooden and decorated with multiple wires.

He is strapped securely to the back.
The guards leave Bundy to think
Alone in the large black room.
There is a flash.
Only then do his eyes show emotion.
At seven eighteen
They are back to nothing.

www.ingramcontent.com/pod-product-compliance
Lightning Source LLC
LaVergne TN
LVHW012128070526
838202LV00056B/5919